Overview

Speaking in public can be difficult. Most people are either afraid of embarrassment or afraid to make a bad impression. To overcome these fears and become an effective communicator, it's vital to acquire public speaking skills.

When we think about public speaking, we usually think of formal occasions like corporate updates and conferences. But public speaking actually refers to every time you talk to a group of people, whether they're friends, clients, colleagues, or customers. Speaking in public is the most basic, direct, and powerful way you can communicate.

Learning how to become an effective public speaker can help you succeed in your career.

Public speaking skills benefit both the speaker and the listener. Audiences learn from you and are entertained when you effectively communicate your ideas.

And you, as the speaker, benefit by leaving a lasting impression of competence and confidence in your chosen field.

This course can help you to prepare effective public speeches. It sets out the preparations you should make before getting up to talk to a group – including choosing your topic and researching it properly as well as writing and practicing your speech. Making these preparations can help you become an effective public speaker.

This course begins by detailing how to select an effective topic for your speech – one that you feel comfortable talking about, fulfills your objectives, and resonates with your audience.

Next, it outlines how to effectively research your topic and prepare for making your speech. Thorough research is the foundation of an effective speech. Also, making preparations minimizes the possibility of mishaps during your speech.

Finally, this course sets out how to write and practice your speech. Structuring your speech correctly and practicing it beforehand contribute toward a successful public speaking experience.

Can you think of a time, with your family or friends, when you were telling a story and every eye was on you? When you were relaxed and the words came easily? Don't you wish it was that easy every time you had a formal public speaking engagement? Most people are capable of communicating effectively in an informal situation. But when a formal speech is required, the same people often feel overwhelmed.

For most people, public speaking doesn't come

Public Speaking Strategies

naturally. It takes practice and preparation to get your delivery just perfect. In this course you'll learn techniques to increase your confidence and your public speaking skills.

You'll begin by learning the basics of good speech delivery - how to start strong by encouraging your confidence, making a good first impression, and building rapport with your audience. You'll also learn how to hold the attention of the audience and finish strong.

You'll learn how to recognize some of the common challenges of public speaking, such as an audience losing focus, being uncooperative, asking difficult questions, or heckling. And you'll learn techniques to deal with each challenge effectively.

This course will also teach you techniques to overcome your public speaking anxiety. You'll learn how to adequately prepare leading up to your speech, and how important it is to relax before you speak.

You'll learn how to get acquainted with your location and listeners and how to focus on your key points when you get nervous. Finally, you'll learn how practicing public speaking will lead to greater confidence.

The last section of this course will give you a chance to practice all you've learned and simulate

Sorin Dumitrascu

delivering a speech with confidence.

You'll practice conquering your anxiety, handling difficult questions, dealing with hecklers, and regaining the focus of an audience that's fading.

CHAPTER 1 - Preparing Effective Speeches

1.1. Selecting a Topic
1.2. Planning and Researching
1.3. Writing and Practicing the Speech

1.1. Selecting a Topic

Public speaking can benefit you in many ways. First, it can help you build your confidence. Second, it increases your visibility, and third, it makes you more persuasive.

Effective speeches require significant planning, preparation, and practice. In order to decide on the topic of your speech, you should first determine the aim, which will depend on the speech's primary purpose. Next, you should consider your audience members and their level of knowledge of your topic. Finally, you should consider the theme of your speech and how you would encapsulate the speech in a single sentence.

Public speaking skills

Many people get nervous before they're about to speak in front of a group. Learning how to best prepare for making a speech can help you overcome this fear of public speaking. There are many benefits of being able to confidently and clearly communicate your message.

The benefits of developing your public speaking skills include building your confidence and making you feel good, increasing your visibility, and making you more persuasive.

Select the benefits to find out more information.

Build your confidence
You may initially lack the confidence to undertake public speaking. When you start doing it, and receive a positive reaction from an audience, it bolsters your confidence. When a speech is successfully delivered, it can make you feel good about your own abilities.

Increase your visibility
The more professional you are when speaking publicly, the greater the chances that people will want to get to know you. This may even help your future prospects within a company.

Make you more persuasive

Sorin Dumitrascu

By acquiring effective public speaking skills, you may be able to bring more people around to your way of thinking. You can inspire others and pitch products and ideas to large audiences. Persuasiveness is a crucial personal asset, especially within your working life.

Consider Jane, who recently started working at a new pharmaceutical firm as a senior scientist. She's never been very shy, but she just hasn't had the opportunity to get to know any of her new colleagues.

Her boss asks her to talk to the staff about quality methods she picked up at other pharmaceutical firms. She prepares and delivers the speech to the staff.

Jane's speech goes well. Her new colleagues are more eager to get to know her, having been impressed by her expertise and experience. This builds her confidence, and she finds it easier to make friends, which makes her more successful in her work.

Question

What are the personal benefits of developing public speaking skills?

Options:

Public Speaking Strategies

1. Increasing your confidence
2. Helping you get a raise
3. Securing a promotion
4. Increasing your visibility
5. Making you more persuasive

Answer

Option 1: This option is correct. Learning to speak in public can help boost your confidence around other people.

Option 2: This option is incorrect. Making a successful speech won't necessarily directly help you get a raise.

Option 3: This option is incorrect. Securing a promotion isn't a direct personal benefit of developing public speaking skills.

Option 4: This option is correct. By being seen on the podium, separate from the crowd, you become visible to your peers.

Option 5: This option is correct. Perfecting the art of speech making can help you become more persuasive selling your ideas to others.

Your objective and audience

Some people seem to have a natural flair for public speaking. In reality, the content and delivery of most great speeches aren't spontaneous. An effective speech takes significant planning, preparation, and practice. When choosing a topic for your speech, you should be clear as to why you're making the speech in the first place. Without this clarity, you may deliver a rambling, aimless speech that nobody wants to listen to.

Mark works at an agency that provides personal assistants to other firms. He has to give a talk to staff members on the theme of new media technologies. Carla, his colleague, is a member of the audience. Follow along as Mark starts to give his talk but is interrupted by Carla.

Mark: Ladies and, um, gentlemen, I've brought you all together here today to tell you all about the something, um, that I think you'll all agree is of the utmost importance going forward within our company. It is an issue, um, which you'll all be well aware of, I'm sure, but it is crucial that I talk to you all about nonetheless. I'd like to begin by saying that you're all, um, welcome to this talk on this fine morning and...

Public Speaking Strategies

Mark is nervous.

Carla: Sorry to interrupt, Mark, but with all due respect, we're very busy today and you really need to get to the point quickly.

Carla is irritated.

Mark: OK, yes, of course you're correct, Carla, I'll just, um, get to the point. Um, what's happening now and has happened in the past in our industry, and in outside it too, is something similar to that movie, with that old actor, um, I can't recall his name right now. But he was a pilot in the movie, and he was training a new pilot, and he...

Mark is embarrassed.

Carla: Excuse me, Mark, but you're supposed to be talking to us about new media technologies.

Carla is angry.

Mark: Well indeed, yes, um, but I'm just trying to provide, um, background to the theme of new technologies in our, um, industry, going forward. If you'll bear with me, I shall explain the technological changes that are contributing toward the, um, development of new ways and means of working within our industry...

Mark is flustered.

Mark's rambling and dull speech has come across very badly to Carla. The most important factor when making a speech is that it has to be engaging. This is regardless of whether the speech is meant to be a funny one given at a wedding or a family occasion, or a more serious one given in a formal business setting.

A speech needs to be laid out and delivered in a way that makes the audience want to keep listening. That is, an effective speech should be meaningful to audience members. This means you must consider them in the speech-making process.

You may have noted that you first selected a topic for the speech – and this makes sense, if it is up to you to choose the topic. Selecting a topic involves four considerations. First, you need to think about the aim of the speech. Second, you should analyze your audience. Third, you decide the theme of the speech. And, finally, you need to encapsulate the speech's topic in a single sentence.

When deciding what topic to make a speech on, you must first think about the aim of the speech. What objectives should your speech fulfill?

For example, your aim in making a keynote lecture at a sales and marketing conference might be to inform the audience of new methods of online advertising, while a speech welcoming foreign business partners might aim to introduce participants to the country and the business at hand.

By establishing a clearly defined aim for your speech, you'll find it easier to decide on the delivery, tone, and style of the speech you are planning. Similarly, these would all differ in a formal keynote lecture in comparison with an informal welcoming speech.

Different speeches have different purposes. The purpose of the speech you're planning could be to instruct and inform. It could be to convince, persuade, influence, or motivate your audience. Or perhaps you might want to amuse and entertain your audience.

Instruct and inform

The purpose of your speech could be to instruct and inform your audience. You want the audience to understand and recall the information you're passing on.

For example, you could be training new staff members in office procedure. Or you could be giving a lecture informing your peers about cutting-edge developments you've been involved in.

Convince, persuade, influence, or motivate

You might be trying to convince, persuade, influence, or motivate your audience. You want your words to alter the audience's behavior or attitudes.

For instance, you could be trying to drum up investment capital or you could be attempting to convince executives of the superiority of a new IT system.

Amuse and entertain

Even in a business setting, the aim of your speech might be to amuse and entertain your audience. This can be difficult as you have to find an appropriate level of humor for your audience.

Humorous speeches are often used when marking a colleague's retirement or at awards dinners, for example.

Sometimes, the purpose of your speech is obvious. Other times, the purpose may be chosen by someone else, or you may have to choose it yourself. There are some situations where a speech's purpose may not be clear cut.

There are several ways you could find out more information if you're unsure of a speech's purpose. If it's part of a regular event, you could ask former speakers about their speeches. If it's part of a wider set of events, you could examine the program of events.

Don't be afraid to ask the relevant people if you're unsure about the purpose of a speech you're going to give.

Consider Marianne, a developer at a media technology firm. She's making the opening speech at an annual industry event. In preparation for the speech, Marianne consults her boss, who says she should explain current trends in the media technology industry. Because she hasn't attended the event before, Marianne asks colleagues what the speeches usually entail. Her colleagues tell her the speeches are focused on cutting-edge technologies but are also quite upbeat, with speakers often speaking lightheartedly about developments. Marianne now feels more confident about the aim of her speech.

Question

Why is it important to determine the aim of your speech?

Options:

1. It helps you when selecting the topic of a speech
2. It helps you decide the delivery, tone, and style of a speech
3. It helps keep you focused as there are many different specific purposes your speech could have
4. It makes you more popular with the audience
5. It ensures you deliver an engaging speech

Answer

Option 1: This option is correct. Determining the aim of your speech is a key step toward selecting your topic.

Option 2: This option is correct. Depending on the aim of your speech, your delivery, tone, and style may differ.

Option 3: This option is correct. A speech could have any number of purposes, so it is best to focus on a single aim.

Option 4: This option is incorrect. Your popularity with an audience is determined by other factors.

Option 5: This option is incorrect. Although it's essential to establish an aim when selecting your speech topic, this is only one step in your preparations. Establishing the aim won't guarantee that you write and deliver an engaging speech.

The second factor you must examine when deciding on a topic for a speech is the audience. It's crucial to bear in mind the audience's interests, expectations, and demographics.

Sometimes, as in the case of an industry convention, the interests of an audience might be easy to determine. In other instances, you might be dealing with a disparate set of interests.

Public Speaking Strategies

You should also bear in mind the audience's expectations. Audience members may have been told you're there primarily for entertainment. Or they may believe your speech is of crucial importance in their working lives.

It's also important to take the audience demographics into account. The audience could be made up of mainly younger or mainly older people. It could be predominantly male or predominantly female. The audience could be mainly local, or a more diverse, international crowd.

You should have a good idea of the professional background of your audience members. Do they work for the same organization as you? Do they carry out similar work to yours? Do they face the same professional challenges?

Try to get a good idea of the audience's knowledge of your topic. Knowing this will enable you to gauge how detailed your speech needs to be.

Finally, bear in mind the relationships in the audience. What is the audience members' relationship to you? And what's their relationship to each other? If it's a small close-knit group that you're familiar with, your speech could be more informal than if it's a speech to a group of relative strangers.

Marianne, the developer at the media technology

firm, has decided the purpose of her speech – to give a lighthearted presentation on recent innovations in the field – and is now ready to analyze her audience. She examines the brochure of the industry event where she'll be making the speech.

She realizes that the majority of her audience is well versed in media technologies. And from what Marianne can gather, as an insider, she will be expected to make a knowledgeable but not overly technical speech to her industry peers.

By speaking to the event's marketing manager, Marianne determines that most of the audience members are in their 30's and are very keen to learn about the very latest development in the industry. After taking this audience information into account, Marianne moves on to the next step in deciding on a topic for her speech.

Question

Which of these factors should you consider when determining the makeup of your audience?

Options:

1. Interests
2. Age group
3. Birthplace
4. Expectations

Public Speaking Strategies

5. Gender
6. Relationship status

Answer

Option 1: This option is correct. By determining the interests of the audience, you can better pick a topic that will appeal to them.

Option 2: This option is correct. The age profile of your audience will help you choose the most relevant topic.

Option 3: This option is incorrect. Your audience's birthplace isn't typically a factor that needs to be considered, unless you're making a presentation on birthplaces.

Option 4: This option is correct. If the audience, for example, expects an in-depth presentation, then you need to ensure your speech is informative.

Option 5: This option is correct. The gender makeup of your audience may affect your choice of topic or your style and delivery. To what extent this will vary depends on the speech's purpose.

Option 6: This option is incorrect. The audience's relationship status isn't typically something that should concern you, unless perhaps your speech is about relationships.

Your theme and message

The third aspect you must consider when picking a topic for your speech is its theme. The theme is the overarching idea you use to tie together your content and make your aim relevant to the audience. For example, your speech's content might be about the latest developments in marketing strategies, for an audience of marketing professionals. And so your theme might be how social media is changing the way marketing professionals develop their strategies.

Sometimes you may have more than one theme to choose from. Consider your audience and your own knowledge and interests before selecting a theme. You should identify which theme has the most relevance to the audience and will interest them. For example, if you were giving a speech to production managers, a quality management theme would likely be of interest to them.

Your knowledge is another means of deciding what theme to pick. You're more likely to speak effectively if you are well-informed about and comfortable with your chosen theme. For instance, if you had to give a talk on innovation, your theme could be focused on innovation in whichever field you have the most knowledge.

Finally, ask yourself which theme most matches your own interests. Enthusiasm is infectious, so if you're enthusiastic about your theme, your audience may respond favorably. In contrast, if you pick a theme that doesn't interest you, there's a risk that you'll sound bored when giving your speech.

It's important you choose a theme that you think matters. Be careful when selecting your theme because a bad choice could undermine your speech. It can be difficult to deliver a speech effectively if you've chosen a theme that doesn't fit your aim and audience, or one that you care very little about. Although you choose a single theme, you shouldn't forget about other themes you've considered.

Marianne decides on a theme for her speech at the media technology event. The speech's purpose is to open the event, and to talk about current trends to an audience of technologically savvy industry peers. Marianne writes down some themes. "The social media explosion," "Revolutionary changes in media technology," and "The digital now" are some of the themes she considers. Marianne decides on "The social media explosion" as her theme.

Question

Which of these factors should you consider when deciding what theme to choose for a speech?

Options:
1. Whether it's relevant to the audience
2. Whether you would enjoy speaking about it
3. Whether you're interested in it
4. Whether you'll be able to write enough jokes using this theme
5. Whether it's controversial

Answer

Option 1: This option is correct. If the theme isn't relevant to your audience, they won't find your speech engaging.

Option 2: This option is correct. The more comfortable you are with your theme, the more likely you are to deliver the speech well.

Option 3: This option is correct. Your knowledge and enthusiasm will shine through if you pick a topic you're interested in.

Option 4: This option is incorrect. It's important for any speech to be engaging, but when choosing a theme for a business speech, your focus should not be how many funny one-liners you can include.

Option 5: This option is incorrect. It won't typically matter whether the theme is controversial or not, if it's relevant to your audience.

The final consideration in selecting a speech topic is encapsulation. You should be able to

Public Speaking Strategies

summarize the main theme of your speech in a single sentence. If you can't do this, that's a sign that your speech may lack focus.

For example, say you're giving a speech about online collaborative tools to an audience of team leaders. Your theme is how high performance can be achieved through the use of these online collaborative tools. Initially, you might decide to encapsulate the theme as "Become high performing and develop online ways to collaborate."

You later refine your encapsulation to "Use online collaboration to create high performance," which more directly reflects the aim, audience, and theme of your speech. Sentences like these get to the essence of what speeches will be about. This benefits both the speaker and the audience.

The aim of Marianne's speech is to describe current trends in media technology in a lighthearted way. Her audience consists of her industry peers and her theme is "The social media explosion". Marianne decides on how the theme can be encapsulated in a single sentence. Initially, she decides on the sentence "Social media is the global trendsetter in media technology innovation."

However, Marianne feels that this a bit too formal and doesn't reflect the lighthearted nature of her presentation. She comes up with the encapsulation, "Review the social and antisocial trends in media technology." She thinks this is a better fit and can be communicated easily to her audience.

Case Study: Question 1 of 2
Scenario

A company's CEO is making a speech to shareholders. The CEO must try to persuade them that a proposed merger between the company and a rival will be beneficial to all involved. The aim of the speech is to convince shareholders of the benefits of mergers, and the theme will be the impact of mergers on share prices. Many of the shareholders are minor investors in their 60's or older who know little about the industry. They're more interested in how their shares will fare than in the workings of the company. Many are skeptical and worried they'll lose out if the merger happens.

Answer the questions in order.

Question

Which of these would be a suitable theme for the CEO's speech?

Options:
1. How mergers lead to share price growth
2. Company successes and failures
3. When mergers go wrong

Public Speaking Strategies

4. Seeing beyond share prices

Answer

Option 1: This is the correct option. This theme would most suit a CEO trying to persuade shareholders to agree to a merger as it would highlight benefits for shareholders.

Option 2: This is an incorrect option. This theme would be irrelevant to the speech's purpose and would not be interesting to the shareholders who have little knowledge about the business.

Option 3: This is an incorrect option. This would be the opposite of the CEO's intended purpose for the speech, as it would discourage shareholders from voting for a merger.

Option 4: This is an incorrect option. This wouldn't suit the purpose of persuading shareholders to agree to the merger as the shareholders' sole interest is in the value of their shares.

Case Study: Question 2 of 2

Given the aim, theme, and audience, which of these sentences best encapsulates the speech that the CEO should give?

Options:

1. "Mergers usually lead to strong share price performance."

2. "Mergers are often difficult and should be

approached with caution."

3. "Mergers don't matter to corporations as much as their corporate structures do, as a strong corporate structure can extract value from merger situations."

4. "A company is more than its share price and company mergers are ultimately of benefit to all parties in the transaction going forward."

Answer

Option 1: This is the correct option. This sentence succinctly imparts the aim and theme of the CEO's speech.

Option 2: This is an incorrect option. This sentence doesn't suit the CEO's intentions for the speech.

Option 3: This is an incorrect option. This sentence doesn't match what the CEO is trying to do with the speech to shareholders and is imprecise.

Option 4: This is an incorrect option. This sentence reflects a sentiment that might sit badly with the shareholders in this scenario.

1.2. Planning and Researching

When researching your speech, there are a number of techniques you can use. You should familiarize yourself with your subject and write down everything that might be relevant, funny, or interesting. You should also think about different ways to look at the subject and talk to someone else about your speech. Finally you should write down five to ten core ideas, then research each point using your sources.

When preparing to make a speech, there are four areas you should investigate. These are timing, positioning, the audience, and distractions. Investigating these beforehand will help you deliver your speech more smoothly and effectively.

Researching a speech

Every effective speech is built on a foundation of good research. You must accumulate the necessary information about your chosen topic. This research can then stimulate and focus your mind, enabling you to confidently deliver your speech.

There are many sources of information you can access when researching a speech. You can consult a library for books and periodicals or search online. You could even interview people in order to glean relevant information. If you're specifically referencing particular publications or people in your speech, you should always make sure to identify your sources.

There are several steps that you should undertake when researching a speech. First, find out everything you can about your chosen topic. Second, write down all the relevant, funny, or interesting facts that you find. Third, look at the subject from all angles. Fourth, talk to someone else about the topic. Finally, write down between five and ten specific ideas and research each.

The starting-off point when researching a speech is familiarizing yourself with information about the subject of your speech. First, find out everything you can about the topic you've chosen, consulting whatever reliable sources you can access. Use a variety of sources and make sure all sources are up to date. As you go along, note any interesting statistics, jokes, or inspiring facts about the topic that you encounter on the subject.

Find out about the topic

You're likely to already be somewhat familiar with the topic of your speech. However, verifying specific facts, coming up with concise and entertaining ways of explaining things, and thinking about the topic by looking up source material, will benefit you when it comes to writing your speech.

Write down facts

Take note of facts and stories about your chosen topic that you think might interest an audience. If you're talking about a specific person, you might choose interesting biographical anecdotes.

For example, as part of a series of events designed to promote high performance in her workplace, Keisha is giving a talk on an historic figure who has inspired her. She chooses Abraham Lincoln because underlying his greatest actions were preparation and contemplation, which she feels are important for high performance. The first thing she does is search online for information on him.

Next, she visits a local library where she checks out a couple of biographies about Lincoln. By searching the library database, she also discovers that a few of the magazines in the library have some relevant articles.

From these sources, she starts collecting facts, engaging anecdotes, and all the other information she thinks could possibly be useful when putting together her speech.

Researching a topic for a speech doesn't just entail consulting documentary resources and writing down facts. Look at your subject from all angles, noting thoughts that the subject triggers. It's also useful to talk to someone else about your subject. A fresh perspective may help you sort the good ideas from the bad.

Look from all angles

By looking at your subject in different ways, you may get a fresh perspective. For example, if your speech focuses largely on the positive aspects of your topic, you could start thinking about the negative aspects, and vice versa. You should also write down the thoughts the subject triggers. These processes are especially valuable when you're giving a speech on a topic that isn't easily researched, such as an abstract idea.

Talk to someone

Talking through your ideas with another person can help you clarify your thoughts. The other person may point out the strengths and weaknesses of your ideas, and help you select a line of thought that will be most useful for your speech. The other person may also have some specific expertise to lend to your discussion.

Remember Keisha? Having researched Lincoln, she approaches his life from different angles. She starts contemplating different elements of Lincoln's life, not just his political career, to get a more rounded understanding of his character and motivations.

To help her separate the good ideas from the bad, she consults a friend who studies history at a local college. Her friend helps her decide which ideas will be useful and which ones she should probably discard.

Question

Which of these are examples of good practice for researching a speech?

Options:

1. Karen is giving a speech on human resources

training so she consults the work library for relevant textbooks

2. Raj takes note of the facts that he thinks might be relevant to his speech on communications

3. Jennifer talks to her close colleague about personal achievement, the subject of her next speech

4. Mike thinks of different ways to encourage workplace innovation, the subject matter of his speech

5. Bernard finds the transcript of a speech online about health and safety and makes a few edits before passing it off as his own

6. Monica uses a single web page as the source for her hour-long speech on productivity

Answer

Option 1: This option is correct. Karen is finding out everything she can about the topic. This is a good research technique because it provides content for the speech and gets her thinking about the subject.

Option 2: This option is correct. Taking note of relevant facts from sources is a good practice when researching a speech – the facts are the focal point of any speech.

Option 3: This option is correct. Talking to someone else can help you come up with good ideas for your speech. They can also lend you their

Public Speaking Strategies

expertise on the subject.

Option 4: This option is correct. Taking different approaches to a familiar subject matter can unearth interesting ideas for a speech.

Option 5: This option is incorrect. Using another's work without credit is not a good practice when researching a speech. All relevant sources used should be referenced.

Option 6: This option is incorrect. When researching, you should find as many sources as you can. Rarely would a single source suffice.

The final step you need to take when researching a speech is to write down between five and ten speech ideas. Your final speech will be structured around these ideas. When you have selected the ideas you'll work with, you can go back and further research them, expanding each point and developing the speech's content and layout.

Keisha comes up with plenty of ideas and, having eliminated some with the help of her friend, she selects her best six ideas and writes them down.

Keisha goes on to expand each of these ideas by going back to her original source notes and selecting facts and stories that fit in with each idea. Keisha's speech is now taking shape.

Soon Keisha has the draft of a speech about

Lincoln, describing why she admires him and his actions. She also describes what lessons she and her colleagues can learn from Lincoln's example of preparation and contemplation. She quotes the famous Lincoln line, "If I had eight hours to chop down a tree, I'd spend six hours sharpening my ax."

Question Set

Success in creating speeches is based on a number of best practices.

Question

Which of these are examples of good practice for researching a speech?

Options:

1. Molly finds out as much information as she can on collaborative learning, her speech topic

2. When reviewing sources, Reggie takes note of all the facts he thinks will be relevant for his speech on globalization

3. Vincent thinks of all the ways he can look at green energy, the subject matter of his speech

4. Preparing for her speech on media technologies, Julia finds out how many audience members will be present

5. Zack finds out if the projector is working in the conference hall where he'll make his speech on sustainable growth

Public Speaking Strategies

Answer

Option 1: This option is correct. Finding out all you can about a topic is a good practice for speech research.

Option 2: This option is correct. Taking note of all the facts you think are relevant is a good process when researching a speech.

Option 3: This option is correct. Examining your topic from more than one perspective can yield interesting ideas for your speech.

Option 4: This option is incorrect. Although tallying audience numbers can help when presenting, it doesn't help when researching a speech.

Option 5: This option is incorrect. Checking the projector's status won't help you when researching your speech.

Question 2 of 2

Which of these are examples of what you should do when researching a speech?

Options:

1. Neil talks to his friend about the ideas he has for his upcoming speech on innovation

2. Marcia writes down the core ideas for her speech on quality control as bullet points

3. Having decided the exact ideas he'll use,

Norman researches each in preparation for his speech on corporate money saving

4. While preparing for her speech on nongovernmental organizations, Maura asks the organizers how much time she has to deliver her speech

5. Kevin writes down pointers for the host who'll be introducing his speech on time management

Answer

Option 1: This option is correct. Running ideas by friends can help you in researching a topic as your friends may identify strengths and weaknesses in your ideas.

Option 2: This option is correct. Cutting down the number of ideas you generated to just a few is a useful research technique.

Option 3: This option is correct. This is the final step you should take toward researching a speech topic.

Option 4: This option is incorrect. The duration of your speech, while important, isn't a primary concern when researching the subject.

Option 5: This option is incorrect. Although giving a host pointers can be a good idea, it doesn't help with speech research.

Speech preparation

Effective speeches don't just happen automatically. They require careful preparation. Taking time to plan your speech in advance will improve both its content and your delivery.

When making preparations for your speech, you should consider timing, positioning, audience, and distractions.

In terms of timing, depending on the day of the week and whether it's morning, afternoon, or evening, you might want to adjust the pace and length of your speech.

Ask the organizer how much time you have to deliver your speech. You need to ensure that your speech will fit this duration.

Consider Lars. He's been asked to give a speech to colleagues in an office in another country. The speech is about the importance of collaboration, and he has a few days to prepare it.

He checks with the local managers to find out when exactly and for how long he'll be making his speech. They tell him the speech has been set for Friday afternoon.

The managers tell him that a couple of hours have been allocated for his speech. Lars realizes he should probably keep the speech shorter than two hours as staff members will likely want to be getting home, and their attention may drift.

Question

Why should you consider timing when preparing to make a speech?

Options:

1. You may need to cut down your speech if a short amount of time has been allotted

2. Your audience's attention level can vary depending on what time of day you're speaking

3. You may be uncomfortable giving a long speech

4. Your speech will be better if you're allowed a lot of time to speak

5. Your audience will likely want you to speak for a long time

Answer

Option 1: This option is correct. If you have prepared a longer speech than is needed, you can cut it down beforehand.

Option 2: This option is correct. A speech on a Monday morning may garner a different audience reaction to the same speech made on a Friday afternoon.

Option 3: This option is correct. Checking the expected duration and cutting it down if necessary

Public Speaking Strategies

will help you make a more effective speech.

Option 4: This option is incorrect. If you're asked to speak for longer than you're prepared to, explain to the organizer that a shorter duration would be better.

Option 5: This option is incorrect. Speeches vary vastly in length. The longer you talk, though, the harder it'll be to keep the audience's attention.

The second area where you should make preparations is positioning. Find out whether you'll have an introduction, whether you'll have a podium, and whether the audience members will be sitting down or standing.

Being introduced can lend importance to your speech and help to create excitement and anticipation. Introductions can also save you from having to ask people to turn off cell phones and pay attention. Don't be afraid to give the host pointers on what to say in the introduction.

A podium allows you to use notes without the audience seeing them. If there's no podium, having lots of notes may seem careless and there's always a chance you'll drop a sheet during the speech.

Usually, you'll make a speech to a seated audience. However, occasionally you may talk to a standing group. People's attention spans tend to be shorter when they're standing, as their legs get tired. It's essential that everyone can see you, so pick an elevated spot to talk from.

In further preparation for his speech on collaboration, Lars persuades the managers to select someone to say a few introductory words before he begins his speech. He has found introductions help make his speeches run smoother.

Lars notes that the room he'll be talking in has a microphone on a stand but that it lacks a podium. He decides to memorize as much of his speech as possible so he'll only need short notes when giving the talk.

He's relieved to find out that the audience will be seated for his speech. He feels it will be easier to talk to the staff members if they're relaxed and sitting down instead of all standing around.

Question

Which of these are examples of preparations that should be made when making a speech?

Options:

1. Ayana checks if the audience will be seated for her presentation

2. A few days before her speech, Barbara finds out how long she's expected to talk for

3. Well in advance, David finds out the date and

Public Speaking Strategies

time he'll be making a speech to his colleagues

4. Mike has a lot of notes for his talk, so he checks that there's a podium in the lecture hall where he can keep them

5. Lillian makes sure there are refreshments available in the hall where she'll make her speech

6. Marvin buys a suit so that he'll look good while giving his talk

Answer

Option 1: This option is correct. Ayana knows it will be easier to keep her audience's attention when they're seated.

Option 2: This option is correct. Checking the expected duration is important as you may need to make final adjustments to your speech to meet that requirement.

Option 3: This option is correct. By checking the date and time in advance, David can anticipate how long he should talk for.

Option 4: This option is correct. By confirming there's a podium in the room, Mike sees he can comfortably bring along all his notes.

Option 5: This option is incorrect. Arranging refreshments isn't a task a speechmaker would usually have to undertake.

Option 6: This option is incorrect. While looking good is important, buying a suit isn't an essential preparation before finalizing a speech.

The third area that you should consider when preparing your speech is the audience. Two of the most important factors to gauge are how big the audience for your presentation is and what the audience members have been doing prior to your speech.

Checking the audience size can help you decide how you'll deliver the speech. You may be able to talk less formally and it may not be as difficult to project your voice when talking to a smaller group. However, you may have to work harder to project your voice if there are many members.

Find out what the audience is doing prior to your speech. For example, the audience members are likely to be less responsive if they're coming out of a long, stressful day of meetings. You may decide they'll appreciate a lighthearted speech after their day's work.

Remember Lars? He's still finding out information in preparation for his collaboration speech at his firm's foreign office.

He checks the firm's online calendar to see how many people have confirmed their attendance. He sees that it's about two dozen individuals. He's relieved, as he feels a small audience will be easier to talk to.

His audience members will be coming to his talk directly after their lunch break. He hopes they'll be relaxed and responsive to what he has to say about collaboration.

The fourth area that you should evaluate when preparing your speech is distractions. These come in two categories: environmental distractions and logistic distractions.

Environmental distractions

Environmental distractions can take many forms. Large windows for the audience to gaze out of, traffic, construction or air conditioning noise, and even the room temperature may all distract your audience.

See if the air conditioning has been set to the correct temperature and if blinds can be pulled down over the windows. The microphone volume may also need to be adjusted to deal with competing noise.

Logistic distractions

Logistic distractions can include malfunctioning or broken equipment, or even just bringing along too many props.

Simplify and discard props where possible. Check immediately prior to the speech whether essential equipment such as projectors, laptops, microphones, and your notes are all present and functioning.

In final preparation for his speech, Lars checks the conference room once more. The room has a big window looking out onto a busy street that could distract his audience. He ensures the curtains are closed during his speech.

Lars also notices the noise from the room's air conditioning. He notes that he'll need to turn up his microphone volume for his speech.

Finally, Lars checks that the room's DVD player and projector are in working order as he intends to show a video during his speech. He finds that the DVD player's remote control is missing batteries and takes note to get some.

Question

Which of these are examples of preparations that should be made before making a speech?

Options:

1. Mike makes a speech with a laptop presentation and checks that the projector in the room is working beforehand

2. Before making a speech to a group of her peers, Melissa finds out what the expected audience

Public Speaking Strategies

size is

3. Spence checks with the organizer whether there'll be someone introducing his speech

4. Bhadrak checks to see if the conference room is clean before making his speech

5. Catherine knows there's always the right equipment in every conference room she makes speeches in

Answer

Option 1: This option is correct. Mike makes sure that a possible logistic distraction is dealt with before he starts to make the speech.

Option 2: This option is correct. Knowing the audience size helps Melissa prepare for the tone she'll use in her presentation.

Option 3: This option is correct. Checking if there'll be an introduction is an important preparatory step when making a speech.

Option 4: This option is incorrect. The cleanliness of the room isn't typically a concern that requires preparation when making a speech.

Option 5: This option is incorrect. Catherine's confidence could be problematic. By not checking the equipment, she risks a logistic problem on the day of the speech.

1.3. Writing and Practicing the Speech

Writing an effective speech is a five-part process. First, you should list the main points to be covered and structure them into three distinct parts – the opening, the body, and the conclusion of your speech. Second, outline the speech within the structure. Third, make the speech engaging by telling a story and incorporating humor. Fourth, prepare a draft and get feedback. And fifth, write the final speech.

There are several practice techniques you can use. First, practice often until you are very familiar with the speech. Second, practice out loud and gain feedback from a practice audience. Third, practice while distracted. Fourth, record your practice and review it. And fifth, check that your speech is the right duration.

Writing a speech

To deliver a great speech, you must first write it. And writing a great speech takes careful and detailed preparation. To create an effective speech, you need to fit your ideas into a logical structure. And your speech needs a clearly-defined opening, body, and conclusion.

There are key steps you need to take to successfully write a speech. First, list the main points to be covered and structure them into three distinct parts – the opening, the body, and the conclusion. Second, outline your speech within the structure. Third, make the speech engaging by telling a story and incorporating humor. Fourth, prepare a draft speech and get feedback on it. And fifth, write your final speech.

As you begin the process of writing a speech, list the main points to be covered and structure them into the opening, the body, and the conclusion of your speech. Then, use this structure to help you outline your speech.

List the main points

List the main points you are covering in your speech and arrange them in a logical sequence.

For example, say you're preparing a speech on

relaxation. You set out your main points about relaxation, such as the benefits of relaxation, types of relaxation, and relaxation tips and techniques, in a sequence that makes sense.

Outline your speech

You must outline your speech within the opening, body, and conclusion structure, drawing out each of your main points. Remember, the body will form the core of your speech. Typically, the opening comprises 10 to 15% of a speech, whereas the conclusion is usually 5 to 10% of it.

For example, you're creating an outline of an award acceptance speech and you place each part of the outline in the relevant sections. In your introduction, you graciously acknowledge the award and express your thanks. In the body, you cover main points like what the award means to you and how the team contributed. In your conclusion, you highlight the values of the organization giving the award.

Consider Reuben. He is writing a speech on globalization that he'll give to his colleagues and some guests. He lists and organizes his main points, and decides his introduction will be about business opportunities that arise from globalization.

He has a point about globalization opening new

doors, which he places in the opening section. His points about increased markets and sales and greater creativity and product innovation are placed within the body.

His point that globalization should be seen as a promise and not a threat for existing businesses is left to the conclusion.

Facts and figures on their own don't make for an interesting speech. So the next step you should take is to make your speech engaging by telling a story or inserting some humor. Some topics lend themselves to storytelling and humor. With other subjects, you'll have to work hard at finding an engaging story. For example, if you were preparing a speech on conflict resolution, you could include a lighthearted anecdote on a workplace conflict about an empty coffee maker.

In Reuben's case, although he has assembled lots of relevant facts and figures about globalization, he knows that the speech is a bit too academic. If he doesn't include some engaging stories in the speech, he's in danger of boring the audience.

He decides to use his own cell phone as an example. He will tell the audience the story of his phone, where it was developed, and where each component came from. He will show how globalization is integral to the phone's existence.

And he'll describe how many modern consumer products can be analyzed in a similar way.

An engaging anecdote such as this might be included in the introduction of the speech, to reel in the audience to the main points as detailed in the body.

Question

Esther is writing a speech on corporate environmentalism. Match her main points to their correct speech sections. Each speech section may have more than one match.

Options:

A. Defining corporate environmentalism

B. What corporations can do to be environmentally friendly

C. A real life story of how important real life environmentalism is

D. The future of corporate environmentalism

Targets:

1. The introduction
2. The body
3. The conclusion

Answer

The points you make in your introduction might include a definition of your terms and an anecdote to hook the audience.

Public Speaking Strategies

The body of your speech might include points about how the speech's topic may be applied to the group you're talking to.

Your conclusion might include a point about what will happen from now on in the area you have talked about.

The next step when writing a speech is preparing a draft and seeking feedback. You flesh out your speech in the draft. Then you get someone else to review it and give you feedback. This may flag potential problems such as sections that may be unnecessary. For example, you ask colleagues to review your speech on communication. One of them points out that your tone is inappropriate for the audience. This feedback enables you to develop a more effective speech.

Reuben drafts his speech about globalization, creating a full introduction, body, and conclusion. He elaborates on each point in his outline until he is satisfied he has a good working draft.

To help him refine the speech, he shows it to his colleague Brad, who reads it and suggests some edits. Brad feels that the detailed history of globalization Reuben has included in the speech won't be of interest to the audience and that he should remove it. He also suggests Reuben include more examples of globalization successes throughout his speech.

Reuben agrees with Brad's assessment of the draft and takes note of the changes Brad has suggested so he can include them in the final version of his speech.

The last step is to write your final version of the speech. This version will incorporate any changes you make in light of feedback you've received in the previous stage. You should refine the previous draft where possible to create a speech that's engaging and flows well.

Reuben is now ready to start writing the final version of his speech.

Reuben writes his final speech with a clearer idea of what he should say and how he should say it. He includes lots of real-world examples of globalization to help explain the phenomenon. He discards unnecessary parts of his draft speech. He also makes sure that his conclusion makes a point that will leave a lasting impression on his audience.

By putting in all the necessary work to write a well-structured, engaging speech, Reuben finds that his audience is attentive and responsive when he finally delivers it.

Question

Public Speaking Strategies

Lori is writing a speech about resource allocation in large corporations. Her main point is that lengthy preparation can save time later. Similarly, she wants to show how there are numerous systems of allocating resources and not every type works for every large corporation, and that some experimentation may be necessary. To lighten the tone, she will tell an amusing story of resource allocation gone awry in a fictional workplace.

Sequence the steps she takes to write a speech in the correct order.

Options:

A. Lori lists her main points – experimenting systems, and lengthy preparations – in their logical order

B. Lori outlines her resource allocation speech and places it in the structure

C. Lori includes an amusing story about resource allocation in a fictional workplace

D. Lori writes a draft and lets friends read it and air their criticisms

E. Lori writes the final version of her resource allocation speech

Answer

Lori lists her main points – experimenting systems, and lengthy preparations – in their logical order is ranked the first step. Listing the main points is Lori's first step in writing her speech.

Lori outlines her resource allocation speech and places it in the structure is ranked the second step. Lori outlines her speech after having listed her main points and placed them within the speech structure.

Lori includes an amusing story about resource allocation in a fictional workplace is ranked the third step. The third step, Including amusing anecdotes is a way of enlivening the speech outline and creating hooks to draw in the audience.

Lori writes a draft and lets friends read it and air their criticisms is ranked the fourth step. This is the fourth step in writing a speech. Lori's draft and the feedback she gets will help her finalize the speech.

Lori writes the final version of her resource allocation speech is ranked the fifth step. Writing the final version of her speech is the final step Lori undertakes.

Practicing a speech

So now you've written your speech. All you have to do is stand up in front of your audience and present it, right? Well, you'll find the old adage "practice makes perfect" really pays off. Once you've written your speech, you should take every opportunity to practice it or you risk making it evident to your audience that you didn't. And the more you practice your speech, the more confident you'll feel when you're delivering it.

Hannah is making a speech on adult education for her colleagues at the college where she works, but she hasn't had time to practice it. Follow along as she gives her speech.

Hannah: Ladies and, um, gentlemen, you're all, um, here today to listen as I talk about um child, sorry, adult education. It is an increasingly important, um, topic. Which, um...

Hannah is hesitant.

Hannah: Now where was I? Oh yes, adult education is an, um, increasingly important topic as more and more adults are, um, enrolling in courses. Lifelong education has, um, become the norm for most people with a professional background.

Hannah is embarrassed.

Sorin Dumitrascu

Hannah: As the great adult education pioneer George Beckett once said, oh I beg your pardon his name was George Birkbeck, he once said that education institutes liberate the mind and of course what he was saying here is that institutes of education, um, particularly for adult learners, are a way of, um, liberating the mind...

Hannah is nervous and speaks fast.

What do you think Hannah did wrong in this example? With regard to her delivery, she sounds unsure of herself. It's important to practice a speech as many times as possible until you feel totally comfortable with it.

The more familiar you are with your speech beforehand, the better you'll deliver it. Unlike Hannah, you won't be hesitant in your delivery or make undue pauses in your presentation. Practicing your speech can also reduce nervousness. Nervousness is a common problem for those who fail to practice their speech, and it can lead to speaking too fast to the audience.

Hannah has also made a factual error in her presentation, something she would be less apt to do if she had been able to practice her speech beforehand.

There are five techniques to follow when

practicing a speech. First, practice until you're very familiar with the speech. Second, practice out loud and gain feedback from a practice audience. Third, practice while distracted. Fourth, record your practice and review it. And fifth, practice to check duration.

Practice until you're familiar
Start practicing as early and as often as possible. The longer you're familiar with the material, the more comfortable you'll be with it and the more of it you'll recall without having to look at the page.

Practice out loud
By practicing a speech out loud to a small audience, you'll think of better ways to say some of your points. It also works as a test run for your material. If your small audience doesn't like something, chances are your bigger, real audience won't either.

Practice while distracted
Practicing a speech while doing other activities, such as going for a walk, can make you think deeper and also solidify the speech in your mind. Distracted practice also prepares you better for possible distractions on the day you give the speech.

Record your practice
Record your speech and then play it back. By

hearing how it sounds, you'll likely notice awkward phrasings and sections of the speech that aren't as effective when voiced as they are in written form.

Practice to check duration

If you've been allotted 30 minutes for your speech, make sure when you practice it that it comes in at 30 minutes, or a little less. You don't want to keep an audience longer than they're expecting, but you also don't want a speech that's too brief.

Question

What are effective techniques to follow when practicing a speech?

Options:

1. Practicing early until you are very familiar with the speech
2. Practicing out loud and gaining feedback from a practice audience
3. Practicing while distracted
4. Recording your practice and reviewing the recording
5. Practicing to ensure your speech is the right duration
6. Practicing only the morning of the speech, so that you sound fresh
7. Have others read your speech to you

Answer

Public Speaking Strategies

Option 1: This option is correct. By practicing early and often, you can become comfortable with the speech.

Option 2: This option is correct. Your practice audience can pick up on flaws in your speech before you deliver it to a bigger audience.

Option 3: This option is correct. Practicing while undertaking other activities is a good way to solidify the content of a speech in your mind.

Option 4: This option is correct. By recording and then reviewing your speech practice, you can notice which parts of the speech are weakest.

Option 5: This option is correct. It's important that you talk for the right amount of time – neither for too short nor too long of a duration.

Option 6: This option is incorrect. You should practice as often as is feasible so that you're comfortable with the speech and can deliver it in a fluid manner on the day you're to give the speech.

Option 7: This option is incorrect. Asking others to read your speech to you won't help you when you're delivering the speech. You must practice yourself.

CHAPTER 2 - Confident Public Speaking

2.1. Basics of Good Speech Delivery
2.2. Challenges of Public Speaking
2.3. Overcoming Public Speaking Anxiety
2.4. Deliver a Speech with Confidence

2.1. Basics of Good Speech Delivery

The first step to overcoming the challenges of public speaking is to recognize the basics of good speech delivery.

Practice your speech to encourage your confidence and give you a sense of ownership over your words. Then you need to make a good first impression – be relaxed and natural, dress appropriately, and make eye contact. From there, you can build on the rapport you have by involving your audience and using "we" instead of "you."

When you're delivering your speech, you need to make sure you hold the attention of the audience by speaking with enthusiasm and clarity. Finally, make sure you finish strong; allow time for questions, and then summarize your key points.

Starting strong

Does the idea of giving a speech make you tremble? Do you hesitate before stepping up to the microphone? If so, you're not alone. Many people lack confidence when it comes to public speaking but you can do something to change that.

Understanding the basics of good speech delivery will encourage your confidence. And being confident will help you make a good first impression and build rapport with your audience. If you want to become an even more accomplished speaker, you can learn techniques to hold the attention of the audience and finish strong. You can use these tools to overcome any public speaking challenges you may face.

Question

Before a presentation, how often do you usually practice?

Options:

1. Never
2. Sometimes
3. Often

Answer

Option 1: You indicated that you never practice when preparing for a presentation. Practice can help

Public Speaking Strategies

you work out any stumbling blocks and become more confident.

Option 2: You indicated that you sometimes practice for a presentation. It's not often easy to find time to practice. But practice will help you own your speech, and deliver it with confidence – and delivery can make or break a good presentation.

Option 3: You indicated that you often practice when preparing for a presentation. Excellent! Practice makes perfect – the more time you put into your preparation, the more confident you'll feel.

The first basic rule of good speech delivery is to practice. This will encourage your confidence. A good speech may often appear impromptu, but it's probably been thoroughly rehearsed.

Also, practice helps you deliver your speech with flair and strength. So practicing your timing and selection of words, perhaps in front of a mirror, and knowing your speech will ensure confident delivery.

Another basic element of good public speaking is to make a good first impression. You should be well- groomed, appropriately dressed, and relaxed, and be aware of your body language. It's important to practice these elements of your speech too.

Try to use hand gestures naturally and move

about the room comfortably. The audience notices not only your words, but also your appearance and actions.

Be sure to make eye contact with your audience. Avoiding eye contact may give them the wrong impression; they might think that you're detached, or not fully committed to your content. Making eye contact and having a conversation with the individuals who are listening to you will make you more believable.

Once you've made a good first impression, you want to add to that by building rapport with your audience.

Be yourself, help your listeners relate to you by speaking with sincerity. Be focused and don't try to be something you're not. Also, try to involve your listeners and relate your content to things that interest them. Use "we" instead of "you" when speaking to build rapport and share with your audience, instead of talking at them.

Pay attention to your pace, remembering to speak naturally. This will help you avoid sounding like a robot, or worse, like you're talking down to your audience.

Consider Chris, who's going to be making a presentation on using social media in customer service at a national conference. He has experience with the subject matter because his company recently underwent a huge overhaul of its customer service management software to make better use of social media. He's been practicing his speech and feels confident in his preparation. On the day of his presentation, he knows the audience will be mainly businesspeople, so he wears a suit and tie.

Question
What are some examples of the basics of good speech delivery?
Options:
1. You practice your speech in front of the mirror
2. You're relaxed and make eye contact with people around the room
3. You make minimal preparations so you don't sound unnatural
4. You create a persona and rehearse as that character so you're more interesting
5. You're sincere and relate your subject to things your listeners already know

Answer
Option 1: This option is correct. A basic of good speech delivery is to encourage your confidence. You can do this by practicing, so you have confidence in your knowledge of the subject matter.

Option 2: This option is correct. Making a good first impression is another basic rule of successful public speaking. Make sure you're relaxed, make eye contact, and are dressed appropriately for your audience.

Option 3: This option is incorrect. It's important to sound natural. The better you know your material, the easier the words will flow.

Option 4: This option is incorrect. An audience will be able to tell if you're being phony. Be yourself, and speak naturally and enthusiastically about your subject.

Option 5: This option is correct. Another basic rule is to build rapport with your audience. Your listeners will be more attentive if you relate to them and speak naturally.

Ending strong

Now that you've learned the basics of preparing and beginning a great speech, you can move into the substantial part of your delivery. To help you successfully convey your message, you can use techniques to hold the attention of the audience and finish strong.

Now that the audience is listening, you need to ensure that you hold their attention.

Make sure you speak with excitement and intelligence about your subject. Audiences react well to animated speakers who know how to use pauses and language to their benefit.

Also, you should make sure you lay out your content logically, and express yourself succinctly and clearly. You want to paint a picture for your listeners with your words and have them easily follow your train of thought.

Once you've made your points, you want to make sure you finish strong. You should allow your audience a chance to ask questions, but be sure to do it before your closing statement. This way, you can set a definitive amount of time for questions and answers and remain in control of your speech. Once the question period is over, you can summarize your key messages and make a strong closing statement.

Think back to Chris, who's making a presentation at a national conference. He begins his speech with confidence and a little humor, which comes naturally to him and helps him make a good impression. He makes sure to make eye contact with people around the room. And he recounts his recent experiences to his audience, including an honest take on how difficult the change was in the beginning.

Then he gives some examples, using "we" instead of "you" to build rapport. He goes into further detail on the actual steps his company took to change its software. He speaks with enthusiasm and an upbeat voice to hold the audience's attention, and he makes his key points clearly without technical jargon.

Finally, he allows ten minutes for questions and then reviews his three key points. He wants to finish strong with a solid statement that shows how he feels about the subject and how confident he is in his expertise.

Question

What are some examples of the basics of good speech delivery?

Options:

1. You speak with interest and deliver your

Public Speaking Strategies

speech with flair

2. You allow five minutes for questions, then summarize your main message

3. You end with a question-and-answer period that demonstrates your expertise

4. You make a speech that only reveals the main point at the very end

Answer

Option 1: This option is correct. Hold the attention of the audience by speaking with enthusiasm, using vivid language, and delivering your speech with flair.

Option 2: This option is correct. Finishing strong is another way to successfully deliver a speech. Set aside some time for questions and then sum up your key points with a solid closing statement.

Option 3: This option is incorrect. In order to finish strong, you should allow a set amount of time for questions and then make your final strong finish.

Option 4: This option is incorrect. In order to hold your audience's attention, make sure your points are laid out logically and your audience can easily follow your train of thought.

2.2. Challenges of Public Speaking

Public speaking has many challenges, but they can all be overcome with specific techniques and practice. When your audience has lost focus, you can acknowledge the challenge of staying focused. You can also change the activity to help them feel revived. Another technique is to inject interactivity into your speech to help your audience refocus.

If you're dealing with an uncooperative audience, you can acknowledge why they're irritable and then find some common ground from which to build rapport.

An audience that asks difficult questions can also be a challenge. Never avoid the hard questions. Answer honestly, stay calm and don't engage in an argument with a combative person.

Finally, if you encounter a heckler, you should deal with him quickly and firmly to retain control of your stage and your audience. Try to consult your audience to present a united front to the heckler. Or give the heckler a chance to leave.

Regaining an audience's attention

Just as practice makes perfect when you're rehearsing your speech, practicing public speaking techniques can help you handle unexpected challenges as well – challenges such as an uncooperative, inattentive audience or a difficult audience of hecklers.

As you may have noted, to prevent losing your composure when you're speaking, you should master some techniques to handle the most common public speaking challenges: an audience that has lost focus, an uncooperative audience, an audience with difficult questions, and hecklers.

If you're giving a presentation late in the day or just after lunch, you may be dealing with a fatigued or unfocused audience before you even begin speaking. In that case, try some techniques to revitalize your listeners before you start:

- • You can state the obvious – that you recognize it's difficult to stay interested sometimes. Acknowledging that people seem unfocused could cause your audience to improve their manners and perk up.
- You can ask everyone to stand and move around a bit. Moving around can revitalize a tired group.

- You can inject energy into the situation by getting excited, speaking with passion, or using humor. Try to prepare a few witty statements you can use to engage your audience.
- A change in activity can stimulate people. For example, you can tell them to write down everything you're about to say – your top three key messages for them to take away. The promise of receiving important information may pique their interest.

Consider this example. Patricia is presenting her quarterly sales results in the boardroom late on a Friday afternoon. Everyone is tired after a long week. Follow along as Patricia uses a few techniques to revive her audience before she begins.

OK everyone, I know it's been a long week and it's hard to concentrate. Let's stand up and stretch a little, and take a few deep breaths before we get started.

I know it's tough to stick with me, but these slides will take you through the quarterly sales results you've all been waiting for. I know the suspense must be killing you!

OK. Grab a pen and a piece of paper and write this down. These are the two most important pieces of information I want you to get out of my presentation today.

Before Patricia began, she recognized that her audience was tired and that it's difficult to stay interested. She asked everyone to stand, move around, and revitalize themselves. Then she tried to inject some energy and humor into the situation. Finally, she made a change in activity and got the audience's attention by asking them to do something different.

Question
What are some examples of techniques for reviving your audience?
Options:
1. "I know it's hard to stay focused this late in the day, but if you stick with me, you won't regret it. Maybe we all need a little snack to keep us going?"
2. "Before we continue, why doesn't everyone stand up, take some deep breaths, and do a little stretching."
3. "Everyone grab a pen and paper. I want you to write down, right now, what I'm about to say – these are the top three things I want you to take away from our session today."
4. "Now we're going to watch a video, and then a

slide presentation will follow, so perhaps someone could dim the lights for me."

5. "Since no one seems interested in hearing any more information, I guess I'll just end here."

Answer

Option 1: This option is correct. You can acknowledge the challenge of staying interested and use humor to revitalize your audience.

Option 2: This option is correct. You can have audience members stand up and do deep breathing exercises to help get them moving around and revive their energy.

Option 3: This option is correct. You can change the activity to stimulate your audience.

Option 4: This option is incorrect. If you notice that your audience is fading, change the activity or acknowledge the challenge of staying interested. Dimming the lights and watching a video may make things worse.

Option 5: This option is incorrect. Ending your presentation in the middle due to an inattentive audience is not the best technique for dealing with the challenges of public speaking.

Sometimes, you may be well into a presentation when the audience begins to lose focus. You'll know that you're losing them because they stop making eye contact or laughing at your humor. Or you might hear people at the back talking. Sometimes you may feel the atmosphere changing, or the energy you were getting from your audience may start fading away.

How can you refocus that energy when the audience has lost focus? Any of the basic techniques you used to revive the audience before beginning your presentation will also work to refocus their energy during the presentation.

You can increase the level of interactivity to keep your audience attentive. For example, you could ask for volunteers to come up on stage to help you illustrate a point.

Or you can ask audience members questions directly, putting them on the spot and engaging them to keep their focus.

Another technique is to use vocal changes such as pausing or changing your tone. Admittedly, most people, upon noticing that their listeners have tuned out, will begin to talk louder. But this tactic doesn't work. If you stop speaking or speak more softly, however, most audiences will notice.

Injecting energy or drama by telling a story, making sound effects, or conveying excitement will also help refocus your audience.

Think back to Patricia making her quarterly sales

report to her peers. As her presentation goes on, she notices her listeners are losing focus. Follow along as she increases her energy, interactivity, and vocal changes to refocus them back to her words.

This is where things got exciting in the last quarter! I was so proud to see these results! Joe, did you ever think we'd reach those sales goals in a single quarter?

Now if you all recall, when we first decided to try the new sales strategies, we were a department divided! Some people grumbled, "This is a bad idea." Some people whispered, "I don't think I can do this." And others – you know who you are – shouted, "No! Never! I won't change!" But in the end, amazing results!

Patricia used techniques to refocus her audience. She injected energy and interactivity into her presentation by speaking with excitement and asking questions. Then she used vocal changes to keep her audience's attention while telling a story.

Question

Which of these examples represent effective techniques for refocusing your audience?

Options:

Public Speaking Strategies

1. A sales manager excitedly asks the audience questions in quick succession and tells them to yell out the first thing that comes to mind

2. A CEO speaks passionately about the company expansion, and asks for a show of hands for how many people are ready for the challenge

3. A supervisor talks louder to drown out the people talking in the back of the room

4. A guest speaker avoids putting people on the spot or challenging audience members to keep everyone on her side

Answer

Option 1: This option is correct. Use techniques such as increasing the interactivity of your presentation and using vocal changes to refocus your audience.

Option 2: This option is correct. Increase your energy and engage your audience to help refocus a fading group.

Option 3: This option is incorrect. Talking louder when people have stopped listening to you rarely works. Instead, use silence to draw attention back to you and then proceed by speaking softly.

Option 4: This option is incorrect. Even though engaging your audience and putting people on the spot may make them feel uncomfortable, it's a technique to refocus them.

Handling an uncooperative audience

Another challenge you may face in public speaking is an uncooperative audience. They may be uncooperative because they disagree with your message or they've heard it already. Or their attendance might be compulsory, meaning they may not really want to be there. There are a few techniques you can use to handle uncooperative audiences.

Disagree with your message

If you have an audience that doesn't share your views, you can try to build rapport and find some common ground.

You must remain respectful of other people's right to a different point of view, while also finding a way to present your point of view humbly and with intelligence.

Find some common ground and build on it. This way audience members will feel you come from the same standpoint but have differing views. For example, your audience may have different ideas on business ethics, but everyone agrees making ethical decisions is important.

Heard it already

In a situation where the audience has already

heard the message you're conveying, you can acknowledge that you realize that fact.

Then you can link some of your main points to the message they previously heard. Or you can focus your ideas in a different direction to provide a contrasting point of view.

Attendance compulsory

When audience members are uncooperative due to compulsory attendance, you can acknowledge why they're uncooperative and then give them some good reasons why what you have to say is important.

For example, you might say "I realize you're not all thrilled to have to attend another presentation, but what I have to tell you about our new process can help you save 30 minutes of effort every day."

I know attendance is compulsory and that makes it hard to get excited about hearing what I have to say. But I want you all to know that I have a few tips based on this quarter that'll help boost your sales next quarter so you get better commissions.

As I mentioned before, some people were opposed to the new sales strategies but we all wanted to increase our sales figures. The next few slides illustrate how we helped each other out, worked through the challenges of learning something new while doing our jobs, and increased our sales.

Patricia tries to win over her uncooperative audience. She acknowledges their reason for being irritable and looks for common ground. Then once she gets through to them, she builds further rapport and goes on with her message.

Question

What are some examples of techniques to overcome the challenge of an uncooperative audience?

Options:

1. Acknowledge that audience members are obligated to be there but ask them to be open to learning new things

2. Begin by stating that even though you disagree about the new pay scales, everyone is pleased to have them defined

3. Run through the presentation the CEO just gave, reiterating each point exactly, to really make the key points clear

4. State with confidence that you'll prove all opposing views wrong

Answer

Option 1: This option is correct. To deal with an

Public Speaking Strategies

uncooperative audience, acknowledge why they're uncooperative, such as mandatory attendance, then give them good reasons to listen.

Option 2: This option is correct. If you encounter an uncooperative audience that doesn't share your point of view, find common ground to build rapport.

Option 3: This option is incorrect. When dealing with audience members that are uncooperative because they've heard the message before, acknowledge that you're aware but that you have some different points to make.

Option 4: This option is incorrect. When met with an uncooperative audience, find common ground and build rapport. Also, always respect other people's right to have their own opinion.

Responding to difficult questions

Another challenge you may face in public speaking is an audience that asks difficult questions. You must prepare for the questions you're likely to be asked. For example, if you find out who'll be in your audience, you can better anticipate the types of questions they'll ask you. Also, if you've given the speech before, learn from the questions you were asked on previous occasions.

You can't anticipate every possible question, so you must have techniques ready to handle difficult questions. One simple technique is to never give a dishonest answer. Always retain your credibility – if you don't know the answer to a question, admit it.

However, never avoid answering a difficult question. Instead, give an honest answer based on what you know, and then steer the speech back to your area of expertise.

Remember to stay calm, no matter how aggressive your questioner is. You must always take charge and respond in a professional manner. If questioners are being belligerent, ranting, or rambling, ask them politely for the specifics of their questions.

Once again, consider Patricia's presentation on the quarterly sales figures for her department. She

Public Speaking Strategies

couldn't anticipate some of the difficult questions her coworkers had for her. Follow along as Patricia responds.

Gavin: Patricia, can you give us the sales forecast for our product versus our biggest competitor over the next quarter?
Gavin is serious.
Patricia: Um...actually, Gavin, I don't have those figures worked out yet, but that's something I'm interested in too. When I get the numbers, I'll let everyone know.
Patricia is disappointed but confident.
Amanda: I just wanted to say that even though you have all these charts to show sales have increased, I still think it's not worth our time and energy to be doing things the new way. We were fine making sales the way we were comfortable with...
Amanda is excited and ranting.
Patricia: Excuse me, Amanda, but what was your question?
Patricia is calm.

Patricia was faced with both a difficult question and difficult person. To deal with Gavin, she was honest and didn't avoid the question he was asking.

And when faced with Amanda's rant, Patricia remained calm and dealt with Amanda firmly but politely to regain control of the presentation.

Question

What are some examples of the techniques to use when dealing with an audience that asks difficult questions?

Options:

1. A conference presenter admits she doesn't know the answer to the question and offers a reference for the audience member to look up

2. A supervisor remains calm and stops an employee's rant by asking her if she has a question

3. A COO avoids looking unprepared by making up an answer that he thinks sounds good

4. A manager engages in a lively debate with her employee, knowing she's an expert in the field

Answer

Option 1: This option is correct. When faced with a difficult question, don't avoid answering it and don't lie. It's best to admit you don't know and retain your credibility.

Option 2: This option is correct. If you encounter a person who's being difficult, remain calm and put a stop to her rant by asking for the specifics of the question.

Option 3: This option is incorrect. Making up an answer can make you appear dishonest to your audience. It's best to admit you don't know the answer.

Option 4: This option is incorrect. Never engage in a debate with a difficult audience member. Try to remain calm and regain control by focusing on the question.

Dealing with heckling

The fourth challenge is perhaps the most unsettling – hecklers. Heckling can be defined as anything that interrupts the speaker and distracts the audience. It may be difficult initially to distinguish between an interruption and heckling, but as you become more practiced you'll begin to recognize the signs. Sometimes it's understated, such as someone shaking her head or repeatedly clicking her pen; other times, it's more obvious, like verbal outbursts.

You can use a number of techniques when dealing with hecklers. First you should evaluate the situation to make sure the distraction is affecting the majority of your audience.

For example, a person sighing once would not be considered a distraction to the whole audience. However, a person who deliberately sighs every time you make a point to show his disagreement may serve as an annoying interruption for your listeners.

In this situation, you should handle the situation immediately and politely. You could probably ask the person if he's OK and give him a chance to step out. Or you could pointedly say that you researched and practiced your speech with care and were specifically asked to present because of your

Public Speaking Strategies

expertise. Then you could mention that if anyone is in disagreement, he can feel free to leave the room.

Sometimes you need to consult with the audience in order to respond to a heckler. This can help unite the audience against the distraction. For example, you could simply ask the audience if they agree with the heckler or if they'd prefer that you continue with your speech.

Remember to remain in control of your stage and your emotions. Your audience will respect you for taking the situation into your own hands and putting a stop to the disrespectful behavior.

Never ignore hecklers – especially aggressive or potentially dangerous ones. They're a threat to you and your audience and must be responded to quickly.

Consider Patricia's situation again. She's already encountered a few difficult questions and comments from coworkers. Follow along as one coworker goes from being difficult to becoming a heckler.

Patricia: So as you can see, our best month was May – just after implementation of my sales plan...

Gavin: Oh, it's her sales plan now? I guess she forgot I made any contribution at all.

Gavin is sarcastic.

Patricia: ...and then sales continued to increase

into June. And you can see that after I met one-on-one with each of you at the end of May to go over the new sales strategies...

Patricia is hesitant.

Gavin: Thank goodness we had her! We couldn't have made a sale without her, by the sound of it!

Gavin is sarcastic.

Patricia: Excuse me, everyone. I only have a few slides left, and I know you're all eager to reach the end of the presentation. How about a show of hands – how many of you would like me to go on without interruption? Gavin, you're welcome to leave if you like.

Patricia is calm and confident.

Patricia: OK, as I was saying, in June you can see where sales increased...

Patricia is calm.

Once again, Patricia used her techniques to deal with the challenges of public speaking. When Gavin started heckling her, Patricia assessed the situation and decided he was disrupting the whole audience.

Then she dealt with him firmly and calmly – she responded immediately, and offered him a chance to leave. She consulted the audience and voiced their opinion, which worked to stop Gavin and unite her with her audience against the heckler.

Public Speaking Strategies

Question

What are some examples of the techniques to use when dealing with a heckler?

Options:

1. Everyone else is there to listen to the presentation and, if the heckler wants to leave, now is his chance
2. Responding immediately to an angry outburst, telling the person she'll have to leave if she doesn't settle down
3. Challenging an outspoken audience member to come up on stage and have an impromptu debate
4. Asking a woman in the audience to leave after she opens a breath mint and crinkles the wrapper

Answer

Option 1: This option is correct. When faced with a heckler, first evaluate the situation to be sure the comments or actions are disruptive to everyone. Then simply voice the thoughts of the audience.

Option 2: This option is correct. Never ignore hecklers, deal with them firmly and quickly. This helps you maintain control and gain respect from your audience.

Option 3: This option is incorrect. Never engage a heckler. Deal with the situation quickly and firmly and regain control.

Option 4: This option is incorrect. You first evaluate if the disruption deliberately affects the whole audience. A person opening a mint would not be considered a heckler.

2.3. Overcoming Public Speaking Anxiety

Overcoming public speaking anxiety can lead you to experience benefits such as building your confidence, improving your speaking abilities, and increasing your interaction skills.

There are numerous techniques for overcoming public speaking anxiety. First, you must learn to adequately prepare. It's also helpful to learn to relax and breathe before and during your speech.

It can be helpful to get acquainted with your location and listeners so you feel in control. If you feel nervous while you're delivering your speech, you should remember to focus on key points of your message instead of your anxiety.

Finally, you should make attempts to practice public speaking. Practice will help you gain experience and confidence.

The benefits of overcoming anxiety

As you prepare to give a speech, you know you could face a number of challenges, such as difficult questions or hecklers. But if you have public speaking anxiety along with these challenges, it makes your preparation even more difficult. Glossophobia – the fear of public speaking – is one of the most common social fears. It's often confused with normal nerves and anxiety, but it's a genuine phobia and can be detrimental for many people.

Public speaking anxiety is often linked to related fears, such as fear of the actual physical sensations that come with public speaking. For example, you may feel your heart begin to pound, your hands tremble, your brow break out into a sweat, or your face redden. Your anxiety may then intensify if you're worried about how uncomfortable you feel, or that others may notice.

Your anxiety about public speaking may also increase due to a fear of embarrassment. You may feel that your audience will judge you if they notice your anxiety. Or you may be afraid that your reputation will be damaged, or that you'll be seen as boring or unintelligent.

Despite all the fears associated with public speaking anxiety, one thing is clear. If you can find a way to understand where these feelings are coming from and how they manifest themselves, you'll be well on your way to overcoming your public speaking anxiety.

As well as knowing what's behind public speaking anxiety, you should be aware of some of the typical behaviors associated with it. Some people, when faced with fight or flight, chose flight, or avoidance. Other people try to control the anxiety they feel, which results in overcompensating behaviors. And the most obvious behavior associated with public speaking anxiety is nervousness.

Avoidance

People who suffer from public speaking anxiety often use the tactic of avoidance – when asked to speak, they find excuses to get out of it, or they become defensive.

If someone asks you to speak, it's important not to say something to her that you may regret later, like "I hate it when you ask me to do things like this. Can't you take care of your own problems?"

Another behavior associated with avoidance is to speak as quickly and for as short an amount of time as possible. This includes answering questions tersely, and it results in speeches that are neither entertaining nor informative.

Overcompensating

Overcompensating, such as rehearsing your speech so much you have it memorized, is another typical behavior of people with public speaking anxiety.

People overcompensate when they're trying to control their fear. They attempt to cover up physical signs of anxiety or hide their fears. However, overcompensating actually often prolongs anxiety or makes it worse.

Also, some overcompensation behaviors can directly lead to poor performance. For example, mentally rehearsing what you're about to say during your speech may cause you to pause for an unnecessarily long time and for your response to sound contrived.

Nervousness

Nervousness can be displayed in the way you stand or sit – for example, shifting from foot to foot or squirming in your seat. Nervousness can also be displayed by the things you do with your hands – like twirling your hair, touching your face, or clasping your hands tightly. Often you don't even realize you're exhibiting nervousness.

Along with identifying typical behaviors, it can

be helpful to understand the underlying causes of public speaking anxiety.

Causes of anxiety can be environmental, such as life experiences. For example if, as a child, you observed adults reacting nervously to public speaking, you may react that way yourself. Or you may have been in a public speaking situation when something unpleasant happened – maybe a negative response from the audience. That experience may now affect how you react to public speaking.

Public speaking anxiety can also have a biological aspect. Some people are shy and introverted by nature, and prefer to watch what's going on instead of taking part. They get less practice interacting with and speaking in front of people. Also, some people are biologically inclined to be nervous. They generally have a number of family members who also suffer from anxiety.

Consider this example. Jill was once asked to introduce the new CEO at her workplace. She made a huge blunder, mixed up his name, and embarrassed herself. Since then, she avoids any type of public speaking for fear of further humiliation. Then one day she is given a public speaking opportunity that could really boost her career.

Question

What benefits will Jill likely realize if she overcomes her public speaking anxiety?

Options:

1. Increased confidence
2. Improved speaking ability
3. Better interaction skills
4. Decreased preparation time
5. Improved audience disposition

Answer

Option 1: This option is correct. People who overcome their public speaking anxiety typically bring more confidence to their presentations.

Option 2: This option is correct. Overcoming public speaking anxiety through practice can help to improve speaking abilities overall.

Option 3: This option is correct. With more public speaking opportunities, people begin to feel more relaxed and gain practice in interacting with strangers.

Option 4: This option is incorrect. Overcoming public speaking anxiety doesn't decrease the amount of preparation time needed before a speech. Adequate preparation is important for all public speakers, whether nervous or not.

Option 5: This option is incorrect. Once people overcome their public speaking anxiety, they're better prepared to speak, but that doesn't mean they

Public Speaking Strategies

can control the mood of the audience.

    Overcoming public speaking anxiety has its benefits, but the relationship is reciprocal. When Jill overcomes her public speaking anxiety, she experiences the benefits, and the more benefits she experiences, the more her confidence grows and her anxiety lessens. Jill's first priority is to practice as much as she can. Her confidence grows as she learns her speech inside and out and is able to deliver it with ease.

    As well, while rehearsing with her family and friends, she finds her public speaking skills improve.

    Then, once the conference date arrives, Jill feels more outgoing. Practicing her speech in front of people also improves her interaction skills. It's easier for her to enter the room and get acquainted with her audience before her speech.

Techniques for overcoming anxiety

There are many reasons to have public speaking anxiety, but even better reasons to overcome it. You can use a number of techniques to overcome public speaking anxiety.

Most importantly, you must learn to adequately prepare for public speaking. You can also learn to relax, to help focus your energy and feel calm going into a speech. Feeling in command of your environment can also diminish anxiety, so get acquainted with both your location and listeners. Learning to focus on key points will help you concentrate during your speech. Finally, try to practice public speaking.

Ensuring you're adequately prepared boosts confidence, and confidence decreases anxiety. To make sure you're prepared, work hard to assemble your speech. Be the expert and speak on topics you're familiar with. Practice both your words and your actions ahead of time. And find the time to do a dress rehearsal.

Assemble your speech

Try to assemble a speech that flows easily. Public speaking anxiety is often rooted in a fear that you'll forget what you're supposed to say or freeze in the middle of your speech. But if the speech you devise follows your natural speaking and thinking processes, you'll deliver it with ease.

You also need to make sure the speech you create is well researched and that any data is correct. As you do your research and fact-checking, you'll also be familiarizing yourself with the topic.

Be the expert

It's important to know your content. If you're trying to speak about something you know little about, your anxiety level will increase. When trying to overcome public speaking anxiety, be the expert – make sure you know what you're talking about.

If you're talking about something you know well or feel passionate about, it will be evident in your delivery. Feeling you have a lot to say on the subject will go a long way toward decreasing your nervousness and boosting your confidence.

Practice your words

Practicing the words of your speech and how you deliver them will help you feel adequately prepared for public speaking. The more you practice, the more confident you feel, the easier the words come, and the more natural your delivery. Also, the more you practice, the less likely you are to make mistakes or stumble over your words.

You can practice by yourself, or with a friend or

family member. This allows you to work out the kinks in your speech and receive valuable feedback. Then you can continue to practice, taking into account the adjustments you've made.

Practice your actions

You should practice in front of the mirror for an accurate reflection of your facial expressions and hand gestures. This gives you an opportunity to overcome those initial feelings of public speaking anxiety. Looking yourself in the eye and delivering your speech will build your confidence and lessen your stage fright.

Try to pay attention to how you move and the expressions you naturally make. You shouldn't be trying to invent new facial expressions – this will only appear fake. The purpose of this exercise is to discover some signs of nervousness you're exhibiting but aren't aware of – for example, rubbing your neck. With this awareness, you can work on appearing more confident when you deliver your speech.

Do a dress rehearsal

Make sure you're able to do a dress rehearsal. Take the time to do a full run-through on site with the podium, microphone, laptop, or smart board you're going to use.

Your public speaking anxiety should lessen just

Public Speaking Strategies

by knowing, when your audience sits down, that you've already done a dress rehearsal.

As you're working on becoming prepared, you can also work on learning to relax. It's normal to be nervous, but you can use relaxation exercises to help you deal with public speaking anxiety. For example, you can sit up straight and roll your shoulders and neck, or flex and then relax each muscle group.

Visualization can also help you relax when preparing to speak. You must visualize yourself as successful and confident. Try to step through your speech in your mind, visualizing how you'll sound, the actions you'll take, and the positive reaction of your audience.

Finally, do some deep breathing just before you speak or if you feel anxious. If you're nervous and get up to speak without taking a full breath, you'll probably run out of breath mid sentence and have to take a gulp of air. You can prevent this by simply pausing to take a breath before you begin.

Another technique for overcoming public speaking anxiety is to get acquainted with your location and listeners before you begin. You should be early so you can carry out your rehearsal and familiarize yourself with the room or stage. It can also be helpful to walk the route from where you'll be sitting to where you'll be delivering your speech.

It can also help to get acquainted with your listeners. If you take the time to meet them beforehand, you'll feel more at ease speaking to them. You'll also find it easier to make eye contact during your presentation.

When you're speaking to people, don't apologize for being nervous. In most cases, people won't notice, so there's no need to point it out to them. Once you get into your speech and your anxiety decreases, you'll be glad you kept your nervousness to yourself.

Make sure you focus on the key points of your speech. Concentrate on the message you're trying to relay to your audience, not on your anxiety.

If you're focused and excited about your message, your enthusiasm will show. That energy will come back to you from your audience and will help diminish your fears.

A final technique for overcoming public speaking anxiety is to get more practice. This doesn't always mean formal speeches – even speaking out in a group or interacting in different ways with people you don't know well can help. The more experience you get in public speaking, the more confidence you'll have.

Public Speaking Strategies

Consider this example. Maureen is presenting a lifetime achievement award to a member of her professional organization. She hasn't done a lot of public speaking, but she feels confident that she did her research and practiced as much as she possibly could. She arrives early, does a full run-through, and mingles with the audience before the presentation starts. She feels nervous, so she does a few deep breathing exercises to try to relax before her name is called.

Question
In the middle of her speech, Maureen loses her place and has to pause to look at her notes. She begins to feel her anxiety increase, and her brow and palms get sweaty.

Which technique should Maureen use to reduce her anxiety?

Options:
1. She should concentrate on her key points about the award she's presenting and the recipient, instead of her sweaty palms
2. She should concentrate on her facial expressions and gestures to make sure she isn't exhibiting outward signs of anxiety
3. She should acknowledge that she's nervous and ask the audience to bear with her

Answer

Option 1: This is the correct option. When Maureen starts to feel nervous during her speech, she should focus on her key points and not on her anxiety.

Option 2: This option is incorrect. Maureen should practice in front of a mirror before giving her speech. However, during her speech, concentrating on her message instead of her anxiety is the most suitable approach.

Option 3: This option is incorrect. Maureen should have focused on her key message and not the fact that she's nervous.

2.4. Deliver a Speech with Confidence

To overcome common public speaking challenges, you can use a number of techniques.

To deal with heckling, you should assess the threat and then respond quickly and firmly. You can also consult your audience and produce a united front against the hecklers to make them back down.

When handling difficult people or questions, you should not engage the people or lose your temper. Remain calm and in control, stop a rant immediately, and ask what the question was.

Finally, when attempting to regain an audience's focus, you can acknowledge that sometimes it's difficult to stay focused. Then you should boost the interactivity level by injecting energy, asking lots of questions, or asking for volunteers to help you.

Delivering a speech

In order to overcome public speaking anxiety, you must understand its causes and the techniques you can use to combat it. And you need to practice to gain real-world experience. As you begin to feel more comfortable, navigate different types of situations, and deal with different people, you'll improve your public speaking skills.

Consider this scenario. You're a sales executive for a company that sells personal protective equipment.

Your boss has asked you to give a presentation to an audience of your colleagues. The presentation deals with adjusting sales strategies. You've had recent success changing the sales strategy in your own department, so you feel you have a lot to say on the subject.

You don't have a lot of experience in public speaking and you're beginning to feel nervous. You want to convey your speech with the confident, assured tone that you normally have at work. You spent a lot of time researching and practicing, and even rehearsed your presentation for your own team last week. Throughout your preparation, your confidence has grown. However, you still feel anxious about your presentation.

Public Speaking Strategies

Question

Besides ensuring your presentation is well-researched and practiced, what else can you do to combat your anxiety?

Options:

1. You can arrive early at the venue to chat with audience members about work and non work related issues

2. You can focus on the topic of your speech, thinking how useful the audience will find these strategies in their sales approaches

3. You can breathe deeply and systematically tense and relax your muscles

4. You can read your speech directly from your notes so you don't make any mistakes

5. You can arrive just in time to make your presentation so you aren't distracted by anything

Answer

Option 1: This option is correct. When trying to overcome public speaking anxiety, you should arrive early so you can become familiar with your location and listeners.

Option 2: This option is correct. It's important to focus on your key points when trying to overcome your anxiety of public speaking. This helps you stay calm and in control.

Option 3: This option is correct. Learning to relax and breathe will help you overcome any public speaking anxiety you may have. Breathing deeply before you begin and actively relaxing your body will help you begin calmly and in control.

Option 4: This option is incorrect. You shouldn't read directly from your notes when making a presentation, as you may sound less engaged and your audience may lose focus. Instead try to get familiar with your location and listeners, focus on your key message, and relax.

Option 5: This option is incorrect. Arriving just in time to speak may cause you further anxiety. Try to arrive early and familiarize yourself with the location and audience.

www.ingramcontent.com/pod-product-compliance
Lightning Source LLC
Chambersburg PA
CBHW031438210526
45464CB00005B/2247